MARRIAGE *A to Z*

Marriage A to Z: 30 Days to Relational Transformation

Copyright © 2023 by Jason and Tori Benham

Unless otherwise marked, all scriptures are taken from the NEW INTERNATIONAL VERSION®. Copyright© 1973, 1978, 1984, 2011 by Biblica, Inc.™
Used by permission of Zondervan.

Scriptures marked BSB are taken from The Holy Bible, Berean Study Bible, Copyright ©2016, 2018 by Bible

Hub Used by Permission. All Rights Reserved Worldwide.

Scriptures marked ESV are taken from THE HOLY BIBLE, ENGLISH STANDARD VERSION * Copyright© 2001 by Crossway, a publishing ministry of Good News Publishers. Used by permission. Scriptures marked KJV are taken from THE HOLY BIBLE, KING JAMES VERSION, public domain. Scriptures marked NASB are taken from the NEW AMERICAN STANDARD BIBLE®, copyright© 1960, 1962, 1963, 1968, 1971, 1972, 1973, 1975, 1977, 1995 by The Lockman Foundation.
Used by permission.

Scriptures marked NLT are taken from the HOLY BIBLE, NEW LIVING TRANSLATION, Copyright©1996, 2004, 2007 by Tyndale House Foundation. Used by permission of Tyndale House Publishers, Inc., Carol Stream, Illinois 60188. All rights reserved.

Scriptures marked TPT are taken from THE PASSION TRANSLATION *. Copyright © 2017, 2018 by

Passion & Fire Ministries, Inc. Used by permission. All rights reserved. ThePassionTranslation.com.

Book (Paperback) ISBN: 979-8-9893418-2-5

Ebook ISBN: 979-8-9893418-1-8

Library of Congress Control Number: 2023919844

Published in the United States by Benham Media

Manufactured in the United States of America

Books are available in quantity for promotional or premium use.

For information on discounts and terms, please visit www.JasonAndTori.com

MARRIAGE *A to Z*

30 Days To Relational Transformation

by Jason & Tori Benham

Benham Media Publishing

DEDICATION

This book is dedicated to all the couples who've sat in our living room over the years seeking counsel for their marriage. You may have come to us for advice, but we were the ones learning from you. Thank you.

TABLE OF CONTENTS

INTRODUCTION

THE POWER OF PRINCIPLES
*"There are three constants in life—change,
choice, and principles."*
– Stephen Covey

The most successful businesspeople in the world operate their companies by a certain set of principles that make their organizations succeed. Think of Steve Jobs of Apple, Warren Buffett of Berkshire Hathaway, Bill Gates of Microsoft, Lori Greiner of Shark Tank, and Richard Branson of Virgin Companies. None of these left it up to chance for their companies to become what they are.

If people can do this with their businesses, then why can't we do it with our marriages? After all, a principle works no matter the context in which it's applied.

Principles are defined as "the cause, source, or origin of any thing; that from which a thing proceeds."

Principles are the roots that bring the fruit. If a farmer wants an apple tree in his yard (fruit) he has to first plant an apple seed (root). God put the principle of *apple life* into the apple seed so that it would produce an apple tree.

God put His principles in place to bring about life and make it flourish. This includes your marriage. The beauty of principles is that they have the power to revolutionize everything you do if you simply abide by them. And they work no matter where you apply them—in your personal life, at your job, with your health, in your core relationships, etc.

Thomas Paine once said, "An army of principles can penetrate where an army of soldiers cannot." We agree with good ole TP! That's why we've compiled a list of our favorite relationship principles—short and powerful truths we've used to grow our marriage and strengthen our relationship.

Abiding by these truths has shaped our marriage into what it is today. The conflict and quarrels we once experienced were transformed into passion and purpose, all because we chose to operate within a set of guiding principles. In this short book, you'll learn how to communicate with clarity, rekindle your romantic flame, overcome negative thinking, walk in forgiveness, manage conflict, and get back the same fervor and zeal you had for each other when you dated.

There's more, of course. But we'll let you discover it on your own as you journey through these pages.

The book you hold in your hand is chock-full of principles that can help you thrive in your marriage. We designed it as a 30-day devotional - one principle for each day. We call it our "nightstand" book. The idea is for you to set it on the nightstand next to your bed and read one principle each night with your spouse before you drift off to sleep.

To make it fun and interesting, we've used the letters of the alphabet. But since there are only 26 letters in the alphabet (so we're told), we added in a few extra principles to make a clean 30-day experience for you.

At the end of each chapter, we added a short "honey do" to help you lock it in. As you discuss each principle with your spouse and complete the "honey do" each day, you'll grow a deeper connection with your partner. In time, as you continue to abide by these principles, you will see the fruit of your labor and experience complete marriage transformation.

That's our goal. We're certain it is yours as well. We look forward to taking the journey with you. Our first principle cranks it up by showing you the secret to attracting and *staying attracted* to your spouse (and no, it has nothing to do with your physical appearance)!

We're in this together,

Jason & Tori

PRINCIPLE ONE
APPRECIATE TO ATTRACT

*"Trade your expectation for appreciation and
the world changes for you."*

– Anthony Robbins

Think back to the very first time you found yourself crazy-attracted to your spouse. Was it when you first met? Can you picture it in your mind?

For me (Jason) it was at the end of my rookie season with the Orioles when Tori's family came to visit me. I drove into the parking lot of their hotel to greet them, and when I saw Tori walking toward me, my knees went weak. Everything started moving in slow motion. I knew at that moment that she had to be mine.

From that day forward, I couldn't stop thinking about Tori. Every single little thing she did I admired… and appreciated. It didn't matter what it was—even the way she said my name, I thought, "Nobody says my name like she does. She's amazing!"

A few years later we were hitched … and crazy in love.

Here's what I discovered—while my attraction to Tori led to my appreciation of her *before* we said, "I do," my appreciation led to attraction *after*.

Being attracted before marriage is one thing. Staying attracted after marriage is another. It all depends on how you think. The most attractive person in the world turns butt-ugly if you think negatively about that person.

Attraction is a matter of focus.

Twenty-plus years of marriage have taught me that when I focus on what I appreciate about Tori, even when I don't feel like it, I find myself more attracted to her.

The reverse is true as well. When I express appreciation to Tori, I grow more attractive to her. At least, that's what she tells me—and Tori is no liar!

The dictionary defines attraction as "the action or power of evoking interest, pleasure, or liking for someone or something."

Read that definition again. Do you want to have the power to evoke your spouse's interest and pleasure? Then a good dose of heartfelt gratitude is the answer.

In our book, *Beauty in Battle*, we talk about adding a little RPA to your marriage to keep the attraction flowing—Radical Proactive Appreciation!

Research shows something powerful happens in your body when you think thankful thoughts and feel the emotion of gratitude. Your brain releases two powerful chemicals into your body: dopamine and oxytocin.

Dopamine is the *feel-good* hormone and oxytocin is the *bonding* hormone. Your physical body feels good, and you are drawn to the person you feel grateful for.

Even better, when you *express* your gratitude to someone, it feels good to them physically and it draws them to you emotionally!

Isn't it incredible how God wired us?

The beauty of the appreciation-attraction cycle is that the more appreciation you feel and express to your

spouse, not only will you become more attracted to him/
her, but he/she will become more attracted to you. And
the more attracted you are, the more appreciation you'll
want to show.

Entering into this wonderful cycle will leave you with
only one question: "Why didn't we try this before?"

So, do you want to be more *attracted* to your spouse
than you were when you were married? Do you want to
be more *attractive* to your spouse than when you first met?
Then … lead with appreciation and watch what happens!

HONEY DO:

Appreciation starts in the mind, so spend some time today thinking of things you are thankful for in your spouse. If you do this long enough, you'll start to feel those amazing hormones start to kick in. Then, express that gratitude—don't keep it in. But be warned, doing this might result in a late-night romantic rendezvous! You can thank us later.

PRINCIPLE TWO

BE A BLESSING

"Don't just count your blessings.
Be the blessing other people can count on."

– Anonymous

Have you ever been so incredibly thirsty that you could barely talk, only to experience intense excitement at the site of a water fountain? What would happen if you felt that thrill—that happy anticipation— and then you pushed the button and nothing came out? What you needed most in that moment, you didn't get.

When you go to a water fountain and push the button, what are you expecting to come out? Water, right? Water sustains life. Without it, we die. But the only way water can come out is if the fountain is first connected to the *source* of water.

The same is true for us. God is our life-giving source. And He uses people to be the fountains through which He delivers this nourishment.

Our goal in marriage is to be a fountain for our spouse, constantly giving that which nourishes by staying connected to the Source.

Here's the simple truth—God wants to bless your spouse *through* you. And you can do this as long as you stay connected to Him.

But there's the twist—fountains don't just give water through the press of a button; they also take water through a drain.

In dating, it's easy to be a fountain. We're so in love that all we think about is what we want to GIVE. But after we get married, a change can easily occur. Our desire to give can turn into an insatiable desire to GET! And we can turn from a fountain into a drain.

The way you become a drain is by seeing your spouse as your source of fulfillment rather than God. This puts undue pressure on your mate to meet needs that only God can meet. When you do this, you become not only a drain to your spouse but also to the relationship itself.

This has been a life-changing and freeing concept for me (Tori). There was a time early on in our marriage when the kids were young and I was struggling with the weight of being a wife and mom. I felt inadequate.

So, after dinner one night, with the kitchen a complete mess, I took a walk around the block and had a conversation with God about it. I told Him how I felt and that I was willing to do whatever was before me, trusting He wouldn't give me more than I could handle.

I came back into the house surrendered and determined to do whatever God told me, only to find that Jason had cleaned the kitchen. My eyes welled up in tears later that night as I took a moment to recognize God answered my prayer through Jason.

When Christ is the source of the blessings in my life, my expectation falls on Him, not Jason (or anyone else, for that matter). I can trust that my needs will be met in Christ and when He uses Jason to meet those needs, we experience a beautiful union between the three of us. I'm left filled with a sustainable and complete love.

Jesus said, "He who believes in Me, as the Scripture has said, from his innermost being will flow rivers of living water." (John 7:38).

The river of living water flows *to* us and *through* us.

God wants to bless your spouse, and He's chosen you to be the fountain through which He'll do it!

HONEY DO:

Think of one thing you can do today that will bless your spouse. Something that you know they would want or like, but they haven't asked you for it. Do it today and watch what happens.

PRINCIPLE THREE
COMMUNICATE TO CONNECT

"The single biggest problem in communication is the illusion that it has taken place."

—George Bernard Shaw

Do you remember the first argument you had with your spouse? For us, we really didn't argue much in dating. But in our first year of marriage, we made up for all that lost time!

Once, only a few months after we were married, we got into such a heated battle that I (Tori) grabbed the keys to the car and took off. This was before we had cell phones and GPS, and since I'm directionally challenged, I just circled the apartment complex where we lived. I expected Jason to come after me, worried about where I was. But when I got back, I found him sound asleep in our bedroom. (*Jason:* I know, I'm an idiot.)

We tell the full story in our book *Beauty In Battle* and how we were able to work through it. But here's the point: neither one of us can remember what we argued about that night!

That seems to be true about a lot of our early arguments. The issue was never the thing we were actually fighting about. The real issue was the way we both tried to get the other to agree with our point of view when we argued.

Our communication during conflict was all out-of-whack.

As we grew in our marriage, we discovered that the best goal for communication is *understanding*, not *agreement*.

This changed the ballgame for us. It turned conflict and quarrels into passion and purpose when we realized that understanding each other and feeling understood is the secret ingredient for relational connection.

When you learn to communicate like this, conflict turns into an opportunity for connection. So how do you do it?

In our coaching program, we teach a 5-Step process we call the "LEARN method" of communication. We did a podcast on it a while back.

Here are the five steps to great communication:

(L) Listen—Seek to understand before trying to be understood. This is the most important step, by far. If you do this one thing, everything else falls into place. The key here is to listen longer than you think you should.

(E) Empathize—Get into their world and try to feel what they feel. You don't need shared experience, just shared emotion. You may not have gone through what they're going through; that doesn't matter. What matters is that you "get into your feels" with them!

(A) Ask questions—Seek clarity to make sure you understand. Once you fully understand what they're feeling, the best question to ask is, "What do you need most right now?"

(R) <u>Take responsibility</u>—This is especially important if you're working through a conflict. For your communication to be effective, you have to own your part of the problem. This is a vital step, so much so that modern psychology says those who refuse to take responsibility have a "character disorder."

(N) <u>Never undervalue what the other person says or feels</u> - Your spouse must feel safe to share anything and everything without feeling like you will diminish or demean them. If they don't feel safe, all communication breaks down.

The goal of communication is connection. If you keep that goal front and center, and apply the five steps above, you'll soon watch your communication blossom!

HONEY DO:

Tell your spouse about the five steps. Pick a topic and try it out. If you do it with a little candlelight and slow music playing, it may just result in some serious connection! But that's up to you.

DETERMINE TO HAVE DOMINION

*"For everything God desires to do in the earth,
He enters into partnership with those to whom
He has already given dominion."*

– Miles Munroe

When we were dating, I (Jason) was a hopeless romantic. I stopped at nothing to do the most romantic things imaginable for Tori. I planned picnic dates, bought flowers, danced with her in the kitchen to slow country music, and coordinated candlelight dinners. I even wrote love letters and sprayed a little splash of my cologne on there just to make sure she got the full "Jason effect." Yeah, I was a total loser (I mean, romantic).

Fast forward five years into marriage with three kids under the age of four and I discovered that being romantic was the last thing on my mind.

At some point—probably between diaper changes and cleaning up from the hurricane that just hit our kitchen—I was struck with this thought: "I haven't done anything romantic for Tori in a looooooong time."

So, I decided to pray about it. But before the words "Dear Lord" even got out of my mouth, I heard God speak to my heart (actually, He might have yelled!).

"Just do it!" I heard Him say.

I didn't need to pray about it or think about it or wait until I *felt* like doing it; I just needed to do it. The same romantic stuff I did back then I could do right now.

So that's what I did. And guess what I discovered? Action precedes motivation.

The more I took action toward doing things I knew Tori would like, the more I wanted to do those things. My heart started catching up with my actions.

In a word, I took *dominion* over my marriage by doing something I knew would strengthen it.

You see, God created you with the *ability* and *responsibility* to do good things for your spouse, stuff that will grow and strengthen your relationship. All you have to do is act on it—even when you don't feel like it. That's dominion.

Dominion consists of two things—power and authority. When God created Adam and Eve, He gave them the power and authority they needed to take dominion over the earth.

Power is the "ability to do a thing." Authority is the "right to use power."

As God's image bearers, Adam and Eve were granted the *ability* (power) and *responsibility* (authority) to take control of their personal lives, relationship, family, and the garden they had been given to steward. Taking dominion is all about using your God-given power and authority to rule your realm.

And this includes your marriage!

That's the thought we want to leave you with today— determine to have dominion over your marriage! In any area of your personal life or relationship where you can do better, do something about it. You have the ability and responsibility to do it, so now just *do it*!

HONEY DO:

Spend two minutes and take inventory of yourself; is there any area of your personal life where you can do better? Maybe you need to eat better or exercise more so you can have more energy for your family at night. Or you need to amp up your alone time with God. Whatever it is, write it down.

Then, spend two minutes and take inventory of your marriage; what can you do better? After you've thought it through, go for a walk with your spouse and discuss.

EXCEED EXPECTATIONS

*"Entering into the flow of abundance begins when
exceeding expectations becomes a way of life."*

– Robin Crow

Disappointment is often the gap between expectation and reality. When you expect one thing but get another, disappointment is the emotion that ensues.

When it comes to avoiding this terrible trap in marriage, there are two simple things to do:

- Learn to *manage* expectations.
- Strive to *exceed* expectations.

Managing expectations is about establishing behavioral norms so you both know what to expect from each other. Exceeding expectations is about doing more than what you've established.

Managing expectations keeps your relationship strong. Exceeding expectations makes your relationship stronger. Doing more than expected communicates love in a very powerful way.

Jesus showed us what this looks like.

When He showed up on the scene, Israel was under Roman rule. There was a law in place that required a Jew to carry a Roman soldier's pack one mile if requested. Many people thought Jesus would set them free from such oppression.

But then He said something startling. "If anyone forces you to go one mile, go with him two" (Matthew 5:41). This blew their minds because they knew to what He was referring.

Imagine the effect this command had on the Roman soldiers. At the end of the mandatory one mile, the soldier would ask for his bag back, only for the obedient believer to say, "I'm going to carry it an extra mile for you if that's okay."

Imagine this soldier walking the entire second mile thinking to himself, "What's this all about?" When the walk was over, the Jew could hand him his pack and say, "I did this out of love for Christ and a love for you."

People didn't do stuff like that back then. Heck, people don't do stuff like that today.

The key to this truth is that the first mile fulfilled an obligation, but the second mile was done out of love.

History shows the powerful results of this type of mindset. Within a few hundred years, the Roman world was turned upside down as Christianity spread like wildfire across the nation.

When we first got married, Tori and I had to learn to set realistic expectations. This is a good thing for any couple to do. But after 20+ years of marriage, we've discovered that while setting expectations may keep you from conflict, exceeding expectations deepens your connection.

Husbands, does your wife expect you to take your plate to the sink after dinner? Try doing all the dishes and watch what happens.

Wives, does your husband expect you to be upset at him because he had to work late? Well, surprise him with a late-night romantic rendezvous and watch how he responds.

If you love your spouse and value deep connection, then show it by going the extra mile. Exceed expectations and watch how your hearts will gel with each other.

HONEY DO:

Find one thing you can do this week for your spouse and then go the extra mile. It doesn't have to be something big. Small things make a big difference.

PRINCIPLE SIX
FAN THE FLAME

"Love is a flame to set the will on fire."
– John Masefield

We love '80s music, and you should too. If you don't, we are no longer friends! One of the best love songs to come out of that amazing decade was *Eternal Flame* by The Bangles. There's a line in the song that says, "Is this feeling an eternal flame?"

The answer to that question as it relates to your marriage is a resounding YES! But that flame can easily go out if you don't tend it, if you don't "fan it into flame."

The love you feel for your spouse is like a flame in your heart. But it's not like the flame of a candle; it's more like the flame of a coal.

Think about the difference between a candle and a coal. What happens when you blow on the flame of a candle? It goes out.

But what about coal (like the burning ember inside a fire pit)? What happens when you blow on that?

It heats up!

The same wind that extinguishes the flame of the candle ignites the flame of the coal. A candle is lit from the outside. A coal burns from the inside.

Love in your heart is like heat in a coal; it's there, but you have to fan it into flame to keep it hot.

I remember very well the time where my (Jason's) love for Tori didn't feel like the raging fire it once had been. I wanted it back, but I didn't know how. So, I began to pray and ask God to show me. Every morning I got up while it was still dark, kneeled beside our bed, laid my hands on Tori as she was sleeping, and prayed for God to rekindle the deeply connected love we once had.

The more I prayed, the more convicted I became. The flame in my heart had begun to die out because I had stopped pursuing her.

The level of your pursuit determines the intensity of the flame in your heart. I had not realized this, and the more casual I was toward Tori, the less passionate I felt about her.

From that time forward, I began to pursue Tori with a reckless abandon, like I did before we got married. And she responded to it. We share all the details, including how I almost punched a dude in the face for hitting on Tori, in our book *Beauty In Battle*. Fortunately, he made it out alive!

The way to fan the flame in your heart is by pursuing your spouse.

Think of those things you used to do before you got married, the things you loved doing together and that drew you close to each other. Do those things again! That's what pursuit looks like.

When you pursue like this, you'll see that the love in your heart is an eternal flame, and you won't need The Bangles to remind you of it!

HONEY DO:

Pick one thing you used to do together before you got married and do it again. Watch what happens in your heart! And, for a little extra credit, light a candle, put on *Eternal Flame,* and dance together in your room. Enjoy your evening!

GET IN THE GAME

"To win the game, just remain in the game."
– Unknown

When I (Jason) was a kid, I played a lot of baseball. One game, in particular, stands out.

We were playing against a team with a pitcher named Brent Murphy who threw the ball really hard. Several of the guys on our team were scared to hit against him. I was one such kid.

Just before I got up to bat, as I was standing on-deck waiting my turn, I decided it was time to get sick! I wanted nothing to do with standing at the plate against a dude throwing a hard object 1,000 mph toward me (at least, that's what it felt like).

I turned to my coach and said, "I don't feel good. I think I'm going to get sick."

He instantly took me out of the game and told me to sit with my mom. But as I sat there watching my teammates do what I was afraid to do, I felt overwhelming guilt.

Faking a sickness that day turned me from a player into a spectator. I sat in the stands the rest of the game filled with regret that I had given into fear and abandoned my teammates.

The result? I was no longer in the game. I could do nothing to influence the outcome. I was a powerless spectator.

Your marriage is much the same. The day you said, "I do," you put the marriage jersey on and stepped onto the field of play. But it's your responsibility to stay in the game—to stay fully engaged so that you and your spouse can win.

A few decades after that little episode on the diamond, and five years into our marriage, I found myself off the field of play once again. This time, however, it wasn't due to fear on the field; it was due to laziness in our relationship.

I found myself a spectator in our marriage and no longer fully engaged in the game. I had my "game face" on at work but I took it off when I got home. Pursuing new clients and putting out fires at the office was easier to do than pursuing my wife.

God got ahold of my heart in a big way and set me straight. We share that story in our book *Beauty in Battle*.

But here's what I learned: God has given us all the natural ability to be good at relationships, but it's our responsibility to stay in the game and pursue a win. We can't allow ourselves to get lazy in our marriage or we'll end up losing the very game we have the power to win.

Getting in the game is all about pursuing the heart of your spouse. We talked about this in the last chapter, but pursuit is so important it bears repeating.

Husbands, pursuit looks like vacuuming the floor even though you're dead tired, planning special date nights, or leaving a love note left on her nightstand.

Wives, pursuit looks like believing in your husband and not giving up on him even though he came home late again. It looks like a big hug first thing in the morning or a text telling him what a good man he is.

Getting in the game is a decision to move toward your spouse and not away. A decision to choose *we* over *me*. A decision to value the gift God gave you and fight for it. Choosing to fight for your marriage no matter how difficult it may get.

I would've crushed the ball if I'd stayed in the game that day. Brent Murphy had nothing on me (that's what I tell myself)! But while baseball is a game that's long gone for me and I can't undo what I did back then, my marriage is a game I'm still in and I can play to win.

And you can, too.

HONEY DO:

Take inventory of your heart and ask yourself, "Am I fully engaged in our marriage? Is there a way I can pursue the heart of my spouse more now than I have been?" If so, do it! Get off the grandstands, jump on the field, and get back in the game.

PRINCIPLE EIGHT
HEAL YOUR HEART

"If you never heal from what hurt you, then you'll bleed on those who did not cut you."

– Unknown

Any time you put two human beings together, at some point, sparks are going to fly. It's the natural progression of relationships.

We say it all the time on our podcast—marriage is the context for conflict.

But what we've found is that the sparks that fly are often a *fruit* of the issue, not the *root*. They are simply symptoms of the real problem.

The deeper issue is often linked to pain from the past. And it's not until conflict arises that what's at the bottom of our hearts begins to bubble up to the top.

It's like a throbbing wound left untreated. Someone may bump into it and you lash out, but that person is not the real problem. The real issue is the untreated wound.

Fortunately, we have an example in Scripture of how to locate and heal past issues that can sabotage our present relationship.

In Second Kings 6, Elisha the prophet, along with a group of prophets he led, were chopping wood to build a new meeting house on the bank of a river. In the middle of the project, as one of the workers was hacking away at a tree, his axe head flew off and landed in the middle of the river, sinking to the bottom.

Now, he could have kept swinging at the tree with the axe handle, but that wouldn't have done much good. To cut down the tree, he needed the sharp edge of the axe. Without his edge, progress ceased.

The man brought his complaint to Elisha. Elisha's question was simple: "Where did it fall?"

The man pointed to the area of the river where it had fallen. Elisha then grabbed a stick and threw it into the water at the exact location where the man had told him.

Miraculously, and to the bewilderment of all, the axe head floated to the top. Elisha then told him, "Now go and get it!"

Our lives are just like this. So many of us are going through life without the edge we once had. Some pain or trauma or sin from the past has taken away the edge God gave us to live a powerful life. Yet we still hack away, growing more and more frustrated because we're not seeing results.

We need to get our edge back.

If we're going to have the marriage God wants us to have, we *must* get our edge back.

Your edge is that special part of you that makes you powerful and strong. It's what makes you, *you*. To get it back, we need to go through the same three-step process Elisha showed us:

1. Go back to the place where you first lost your edge.

    Getting to the root is all about remembering back to pain from the past. A time when something painful happened to you, or possibly when you caused someone else pain. It could also be a sin from the past that caused you to lose that special part of you and now you feel powerless.

2. Bring the cross of Christ into the picture.

Many Bible scholars believe the stick Elisha used was the same type of wood from which the cross was made. If we caused pain through our own sin, we repent, make things right, and get back on track. If pain was inflicted on us, then we walk through the steps of forgiveness and re-process the situation through the cross of Christ. (See Chapter 21 *Understand Unforgiveness* for help processing forgiveness)

3. Watch the miraculous take over.

For an iron axe head to float on water, it took a miracle. When you go back to the place where you lost your edge and you bring the cross of Christ into the picture, the supernatural takes over and a miracle occurs. God will supernaturally begin to do things in your life and relationship that were impossible before you allowed Him to take over.

God has given you the edge you need to live a powerful life and experience a wonderful marriage. But it will require you to process any potential pain from the past. When you do, watch God's supernatural power invade your relationship.

HONEY DO:

Spend some time alone and ask God if there's any area of your life or relationship where you've lost your edge. Ask your spouse if they see any area where you may have lost it. Then, walk through the three steps above.

PRINCIPLE NINE
INITIATE INTIMACY

*"The purpose of an intimate relationship is not that it
be a place where we can hide from our weaknesses,
but rather where we can safely let them go."*

– Marianne Williamson

Have you ever stopped to consider that Adam had undiluted fellowship with God in the Garden and yet it wasn't enough to fill the void in his heart?

God recognized it, of course, because He made him that way. God purposefully wove Adam together so that He alone was *not* all that Adam needed.

Adam + God = *not* good.

Adam + Eve + God = very good!

This doesn't mean every person should get married. But it does mean that we should all be connected to other people. We weren't meant to go it alone.

Here's a shocking thought: God is not all you need! You need other people. And as a married person, you need your spouse! Desperately.

God created you that way on purpose. Why? So that you could experience something that only a relationship with co-equals can give you—*intimacy*.

Intimacy is *to be fully known and fully accepted*. It's what gives us a deep connection with others, provides a sense of belonging, and makes us one. And when we are one, we fully reflect the image of God.

Apart from the deep sense of connection that only intimacy can bring, especially in the context of marriage, we are left with a void that cannot be filled any other way.

The late Tim Keller wrote this about intimacy: "To be loved but not known is comforting but superficial. To be known and not loved is our greatest fear. But to be fully known and truly loved is, well, a lot like being loved by God. It is what we need more than anything. It liberates us from pretense, humbles us out of our self-righteousness, and fortifies us for any difficulty life can throw at us."

But intimacy doesn't happen on its own. You have to work at it. In a word, you need to *initiate* it. How do we do that? Try these four steps:

- **Seek to know your spouse.** Become a student of your partner. Never stop asking questions. Be in a constant state of discovery, always looking for gold.

- **Seek to be known by your spouse.** Vulnerability is the most attractive trait in marriage. Without it, there's no real connection. Open up and let them in!

- **Be accepting of your spouse.** Fully accept your partner, warts and all! This will release them from the feeling they must measure up to get your approval.

- **Accept yourself.** Know that God made you just the way you are and that He likes you that way. Don't let the fear of rejection keep you from true intimacy.

Intimacy is the lifeblood of a marriage. But it won't happen by accident; you have to initiate it! Put away the distractions and focus on each other. Because an intimate couple is a connected couple.

HONEY DO:

Take a walk with each other and discuss these four questions:

- Are you comfortable being vulnerable with your spouse?
- Do you accept your spouse unconditionally?
- Do you feel accepted?
- Do you accept yourself ?

JUMP FOR JOY

"Joy and pain, they are but two arteries of the one heart that pumps through all those who don't numb themselves to really living."

– Ann Voskamp

Every Saturday, we hit a team workout at our local CrossFit gym where a bunch of crazies get together to put ourselves through pain. Above the door is a sign that sums up this whacky mindset: "I hate you. I hate this place. See you tomorrow."

We put ourselves through grueling workouts every Saturday because of the feeling we have when we're done. It's a feeling of total, physical peace and rest. True relaxation.

By the time we finish, every person in the gym is lying on the floor lost in a collective "ahhh" ensation. Then we high-five each other as we walk out the door.

God made our bodies to function this way. To keep us coming back for more, He put some incredible hormones in our bodies called endorphins, which are released after we experience pain.

Endorphins are little messengers in our bodies that block pain and give us a feeling of complete and total well-being. So when we do hard things—like a tough workout—these friendly critters reward us with a brief feeling of pure joy as a reward for the pain we just endured.

Athletes call it the "runner's high." It's what helps you break through barriers and keep pushing when it hurts.

There are many days that we don't want to work out. We'd rather stay in bed and be lazy. But the hope of a reward—that euphoric high—pulls us out of bed to suffer the heat or brave the cold.

Christ's life is the greatest example of this. How was He able to endure the most grueling death any human being ever suffered? By focusing on the *joy* on the other side.

Hebrews 12:2 tells us, "Who for the *joy* set before Him *endured* the Cross."

Jesus didn't "want" to go through the incredible pain of the Cross, but He did it because of the joy that awaited Him—and us—on the other side.

This is what "jumping for joy" in your marriage is all about—recognizing that the joy of your relationship is only found when you're willing to embrace the pain that comes, too.

When you face and endure difficulties and challenges—the trying times that can either tear you apart or draw you together—that's the path to joy in your relationship.

The key lies in your willingness to embrace it.

A few years ago, we got into a fight. I (Jason) was far too aggressive verbally and made Tori cry. In the middle of it, she yelled back at me and got right up in my face.

I was totally caught off guard. I had never seen her act like that before. But at that moment, my heart broke for her. I realized I had pushed her to this point. I made her feel like I was an enemy she needed to protect herself against instead of a friend to whom she could entrust herself.

Thankfully, we were able to work through it. But it was a defining moment for us. We saw sides of each other we hadn't seen before, even after being together for more than 20 years.

She saw insecurities in me, and while she didn't like them, it made her want to draw close to me to help me through. I saw a fighter in her, and it made me even more attracted to her (odd, right?).

For both of us, we found ourselves experiencing a real peace with one another on the other side of this painful experience.

Our hope for you isn't that you will find something to fight over; it's that you'll learn to draw close to each other after a fight. Because when you're in a committed, God-centered marriage, rest assured joy will be on the other side of your pain.

Keep your sights set on that joy. Jesus did it, and so can you.

HONEY DO:

Think of a time in your relationship when you experienced some type of pain or conflict, and, as a result, you drew closer to each other because of it. Make a commitment that you'll do that with other trials that come your way in the future.

KILL THE KRAZY

"Some people can't tell they're annoying.
Which is even more annoying."

– Unknown

If any part of your behavior drives your spouse crazy, stop it! If you do anything that grates their every nerve, quit!

You've gotta "kill the krazy!"

Yes, we know the word "crazy" doesn't start with a "k." But we had to stick with our alphabet vibe, so we went with it.

There's an old TV comedy skit with Bob Newhart playing the role of a psychologist that outlines this concept perfectly.

A woman who has a fear of being buried alive in a box comes in for a session on how to overcome this paralyzing phobia. Dr. Bob explains that her problem can be resolved with two simple words:

"STOP IT!"

Needless to say, this doesn't sit well with her. Clearly agitated, the woman told him she didn't like his type of therapy. His gruff prescription for her problem was not what she was looking for.

After going back and forth with each other a few times, and recognizing that he wasn't getting through, Dr. Bob finally cut to the chase.

"Alright," he said. "Let me give you ten words I think will clear everything up for you." "STOP IT OR I'LL BURY YOU ALIVE IN A BOX!"

While we're not suggesting that you talk to each other like this, we do suggest you talk to *yourself* like it.

When you get married, you learn quickly what it is that agitates your spouse. Our advice echoes Dr. Bob's—STOP IT!

Just quit.

It doesn't matter if it's something you did your entire life. If your behavior agitates your life partner, stop doing it.

We understand that there are some things you can't control. We get it. But if you can control it, and it's something that bothers your spouse, stop it.

Understand this: killing the krazy is about changing your own behavior, not forcing your spouse to change theirs.

He/she may do some pretty annoying things, but you can't control that. You *can* control yourself. When we first got married, I (Jason) never knew how agitating my independent spirit was to Tori.

That is, until three months after we said, "I do."

I decided to invite a buddy of mine over for dinner one night without asking her. The moment I walked through the door, I discovered, to my horror, a candlelit dinner for two set in our living room.

What a bonehead I was!

I'll never forget the look on her face when we walked in the door. Surprise, frustration, agitation, hurt—you name it, her eyes said it.

She gathered herself, calmly added another plate, and sat down for dinner with her idiot husband and his third-wheel friend.

Although it took several years and more bonehead blunders, I finally learned to just "stop it"—to quit acting like an independent single dude.

But there's a balancing truth to this concept. While there may be things your spouse does that agitate you, sometimes it's not their job to stop it but your job to accept it.

Throughout the Bible, we find balancing truths. Proverbs 26:4-5 says two things that seemingly contradict themselves: "Do not answer a fool according to his folly, or you yourself will be just like him. Answer a fool according to his folly, or he will be wise in his own eyes."

There are times to be quiet, and there are times to speak up. Those truths balance each other. In your marriage, there are times to "stop it" and times to "accept it."

We share a story in our book and have talked about it on our podcast how for the first few years of marriage, I couldn't stand how Tori left her drawers open. She literally had a mental block when it came to pushing drawers back in. And since I'm slightly OCD, my brain was short-circuiting.

I had some deep conversations with God about this. "Lord, why did you make her this way? Is this some kind of sick joke?"

Tori tried to accommodate my "need" for pushed-in-drawers, but with four small kiddos and her mind scattered in a million directions, we were dealing with a 50/50 success rate (make that 20/80).

God bless her for her effort. Her laid-back personality just didn't care about drawers when there were a lot more important things in life to worry about!

Finally, I heard God's gentle whisper in my spirit, "Why don't you just accept her like I made her?"

I was convicted and chose that day to stop focusing on my *agitation* and start focusing on my *admiration*.

So, when it comes to the agitating behavior of your spouse, don't try to control it; learn to accept it. But when it comes to your own agitating behavior, stop it …

… Stop it right now or we'll bury you alive in a box!

HONEY DO:

Ask your spouse if there's anything you do that drives them crazy, or if they don't particularly like when you do. Commit to them that you will do everything in your power to stop it!

LOOK TO THE LORD

"Look to the Lord and His strength;
Seek His face always."

– Psalms 105:4

Your spouse was never meant to meet your needs. God is the One who does that. And He uses people—your spouse included—as His mechanism through which He meets them.

Your job as a married person is to see *through* your spouse *to* God. God is the source. Your spouse cannot, and *should not*, be your source.

Marriages are falling apart today because people are looking to their spouses to meet needs only God can meet. So, when their spouse proves incapable of filling that void in their heart, their whole world falls apart, along with the marriage.

Our good friend Dr. Kathy Koch explains that all human beings have five core needs:

- Security—who can I trust?
- Identity—who am I?
- Belonging—who wants me?
- Purpose—why am I alive?
- Competence—what can I do well?

These core needs build on each other. Until you answer the question of security, you will never discover your identity. And if you don't know who you are, then you'll never know where you belong, which negates your ability to know why you're alive or what you were born to do.

Everything hinges on security.

You cannot find your ultimate security in people no matter how amazing they may be. You can find a *level* of security in them, but you cannot find your *ultimate* security in them, not even your spouse.

Why? Because people are fallible. And if you've found your ultimate security in someone other than

God, when that person fails you—and they will— your world falls apart.

Your spouse can't handle the pressure associated with meeting all your needs. But God can, and He'll use your spouse to make it happen.

Jesus tells us, "Do not let your hearts be troubled; believe in God, believe also in Me." (John 14:1) The phrase *believe in God* means to trust Him, to commit yourself to Him. After all, He is the security for which our soul longs. When we place our trust in Him and *look to the Lord* to meet our needs, people can let us down, yet our security stays intact.

Upon that foundation, look at how our five core needs are met in God:

- Security: I can trust God because He has never and will never fail me.
- Identity: I am a child of God because He's my Father.

- Belonging: God wants me because I'm His kid.
- Purpose: I want to bring my Father glory in all that I do.
- Competence: I can do anything God asks me to do because He'll do it through me.

God will meet all your needs. He uses people to do it. Your spouse is His top choice.

The question is, will you look through your spouse to Him and give God the credit He deserves? If you take two individuals in a relationship who have their ultimate needs met in Christ, and they recognize each other as simply the conduits through which God meets those needs, you will discover a marriage so powerful nothing can stand against it.

That's a marriage you can have.

HONEY DO:

Take a moment to do a little inventory. Have you been looking to your spouse to meet needs only God can truly meet? Has that put too much pressure on them and therefore strained your relationship?

Now flip the script. Has your spouse been looking to you rather than God? Discuss these questions with your partner.

MOVE TOWARD
YOUR MATE

*"One of the greatest predictors of a relationship's success
is the ability to turn toward each other."*

– Dr. John Gottman

Dr. John Gottman, world-renowned researcher for all things marriage, conducted a study with newlyweds over a span of six years, during which time many of the couples got divorced.ii The ones that stayed together, however, had one thing in common—they *turned toward each other rather than away*.

Moving toward your spouse is about pursuing each other when it's not easy, refusing to let conflict create distance, reaching out to show affection, doing little things to show you care, etc. And it's about responding positively to your partner when they move toward you.

But that's not always an easy thing to do.

I (Tori) have discovered the power of moving toward Jason rather than away, even when it's hard. We'll get into a disagreement and end up later that night lying in bed facing opposite directions, not saying a word. Then I'll put my hand on his back, looking to draw him back in. When I move toward him like that, even when I don't want to, it breaks down the wall between us and Jason emerges from his little cave.

In an earlier chapter we talked about the only way you'll do difficult things in your marriage is to focus on the joy that's on the other side.

But do you know where that joy comes from? It springs from the transformation you experience when you lean into something difficult rather than turning away.

We've seen how this works firsthand. God literally transformed me (Jason) into the polar opposite of what I used to be. And it had everything to do with my love language.

Have you ever read the book, *The Five Love Languages*, by Dr. Gary Chapman? It's a must-read for married couples. Quite simply, Gary teaches that there are five distinct ways people "feel" loved, which he calls "love languages."

The five are:

- Words of Affirmation
- Physical Touch
- Quality Time
- Acts of Service
- Gifts

I (Jason) am a *physical touch* and *words of affirmation* guy. If Tori puts her arms around me and tells me she's proud of me, I feel like I could rope the moon.

Tori is a *quality time* and *acts of service* girl. If I take a walk around the block with her and then help clean the kitchen, she "feels" my love and it warms her heart.

Quality time was always dead last on my love-language list. My natural independence didn't lean toward spending long periods of time with anyone under any circumstance!

When we were dating, I didn't have any problem spending quality time with Tori. But once we were married, it became a chore. I was building a business and had lots of important stuff to do (or so I thought).

The more I focused on how much I didn't want to do it, though, the more distant I drew from her and the more unloved she felt.

It wasn't until I realized that if I wanted to keep her heart, I needed to do the very thing that was naturally difficult for me to do—spend quality time.

I needed to move toward her rather than away.

So, I chose to start coming home from the office a little earlier than normal, even when I could've easily knocked out a few more emails or made some calls.

And guess what happened? The more I *chose* to spend quality time with Tori, the more I *wanted* to spend time with her.

Once I pushed through the difficulty of doing something against my personality, God took over and started the transformation process.

Matthew 6:21 was coming true right before my very eyes: "For where your treasure is, there your heart will be also." God was transforming me as I moved toward Tori.

A few months ago, I decided to take Dr. Gary's Five Love Languages quiz. Bet you can't guess what my #1 Love Language is now! ☺

Quality Time.

If God did that with me, I know He'll do it with you. All you have to do is give it a shot. Move toward your mate and watch what happens.

HONEY DO:

Find a creative way to move toward your spouse today. Maybe a little love note on the mirror in the bathroom, a short "thinking of you" text in the middle of the day, a hand-hold as you fall asleep tonight. Pick something, even if you're experiencing distance right now, and choose to move toward your mate.

PRINCIPLE FOURTEEN
NEGATE NEGATIVITY

*"Relationships with negative people are simply
tedious encounters with porcupines."*

– Shannon L. Alder

Research shows that negative thinking literally destroys your brain. It also wreaks havoc on every other area of your life, especially your marriage.

In his book *The Seven Principles That Make Marriage Work*, Dr. John Gottman shares in-depth research on what makes relationships work and what destroys them. Guess what he found to be the number one killer of all marriages?

CONTEMPT!

Contempt is negative thinking toward your spouse where you put yourself in a superior position. And the sign that you have it in your heart is *comparison*.

A contemptuous spouse says, "You came home late again. You're always late. If *you* were the one making dinner, *I'd* never be late."

A statement like this puts your partner in a defensive position and escalates the conflict. Even if the comparison were true (which it most likely is), focusing on it will damage your relationship.

Contempt infiltrates your marriage through unchecked criticism in your mind. Over time, critical thoughts of your spouse make you feel that you are better than them. And when this happens, it's a sure sign that your marriage is entering dangerous territory.

It works like this:

- Conflict—an agitation or offense sparks a negative feeling.
- Critique—you begin to analyze and evaluate your spouse through a negative grid.
- Criticize—you foster a critical attitude toward your spouse and think mostly of their faults.
- Contempt—you elevate yourself, claiming your behavior as better than theirs.

Contempt fuels pride. And the Bible says multiple times that "God resists the proud." You don't want God resisting your efforts in marriage.

To break from this destructive cycle, you simply need to reverse the pattern:

- Recognize conflict as God's way of drawing you together, not tearing you apart.
- Refuse to think negatively toward your spouse when conflict happens.
- Focus on your spouse's positive traits and build on those, rather than analyzing through a negative grid.
- Refuse to compare yourself, period.

Once you've gone through this process, it's time to work through the conflict. When you do, consider starting with an "I" statement rather than a "You" statement.

Doing this will disarm the situation while keeping you out of the contemptuous zone. It might sound like this:

"I feel like when you come home late, you're putting work over family. I'm grateful for your hard work and the way you provide, but it hurts my heart when we can't spend that time together. Can you make an adjustment to be home on time?"

This statement makes the point but adds a positive element and does not compare, which de- escalate the situation and keeps your heart from falling into comparison.

Contempt puts a stranglehold on your relationship and won't let go until you're left with broken hearts and a broken marriage.

But it doesn't have to be this way. You have the power to break its destructive force in your life. Negate negativity and expect a better relationship as a result.

HONEY DO:

Think about a situation that seems to be a perpetual conflict for you and your spouse. It can be something small, but that you both think and act differently on. Does your mind drift to comparison? Do you think "Why can't he/she do it like I do?" This is natural, but not healthy. Discuss with your spouse, then commit to practice better thinking.

OVERCOME THROUGH ONENESS

*"The oneness of human beings is the basic
ethical thread that holds us together."*

– Muhammad Yunus

The foundational concept of our first book, *Beauty in Battle,* is this: we are in a spiritual battle and your marriage was created in the context of this fight. When you choose to fight *alongside* your spouse in a spiritual battle rather than *against* them in a personal war, fighting together will draw you together.

How is this possible? How can we win a spiritual fight and draw closer together at the same time? It's possible because of the power of *oneness*.

Oneness to Satan is like kryptonite to Superman; he cannot overcome it. It also acts like glue, helping you and your spouse stick together.

The power of oneness is derived from the presence of God. "For where two or more are gathered in My name, I am there in their midst." (Matthew 18:20)

God gives this power to His church. And the most organic form of church is your marriage ("two or more").

When the church (you and your spouse) is unified *as one* in the name of Jesus, Satan cannot defeat you.

The church is God's chosen weapon to defeat Satan on this earth. As Jesus stated, "... On this rock I will build my *church*, and the gates of hell shall not prevail against it." (Matthew 16:18)

Satan will attack you, but he won't beat you. And you'll draw closer in the process.

In the movie *Gladiator*, there's an epic scene where Maximus and his band of roughshod warriors defeat the Roman gladiators. Maximus would yell "as one" each time a gladiator came for an attack. So long as they stayed together, not only could they defend themselves, but they could defeat their enemy. And they drew close to each other as a result.

Such is the power of oneness.

We have a term in our relationship we use for our oneness—*us*. There are times when we'll get into an argument and then one of us will say, "I want to be back in *us*." That simple statement reminds us what we really want and gets us moving in that direction.

Consider this analogy: your marriage is like cookie dough. You've got all these different ingredients that can stand alone but *they weren't meant to.*

Can you imagine eating a spoonful of flour? How 'bout a teaspoon of vanilla? Maybe a bite of butter? Or a cup of sugar?

These ingredients were not meant to be eaten on their own. They were meant to be mixed together. What happens when you put them in a bowl and blend them up?

They become something together they can't be on their own. They are better *as one*.

God is the baker. The bowl is conflict. You and your spouse are the ingredients.

God puts you into the bowl of conflict and mixes you up. His goal is to whip you into something stronger and better together than you are on your own.

But here's the key—raw ingredients don't stick together without a bonding agent, something that can make them stick together *as one*.

In the case of cookies, the bonding agent is eggs. In the case of marriage, it's the Holy Spirit. When two people, fully surrendered to God, commit to each other in the name of God, the Holy Spirit enters the mix and the two become one.

And when two people become one, they become the church, which has all the power in heaven and on earth to defeat the enemy and grow close at the same time.

That's the incredible power you have through *oneness*.

Now, go and enjoy yourself some cookies! And, if you're like us, you'll eat a bit of the dough, too.

HONEY DO:

Becoming one with your spouse is all about accepting each other's strengths and weaknesses as a part of your unique chemistry. Talk with your spouse about how you make each other better. This is a feel-good exercise. Enjoy!

PRACTICE PRESENCE

"Absence sharpens love. Presence strengthens it."
– Benjamin Franklin

The greatest gift you can give your spouse is yourself. I (Jason) saw this lived out in my mom shortly before she passed away in the fall of 2017. It was the most painful experience I've ever been through. But the example she gave will forever live on in my heart and mind.

She died of a lung disease that came on fast. From the day she was diagnosed to the day she died was less than two weeks. During that time, she struggled to breathe as her lungs could hold no more than about 60-70% of normal oxygen levels.

She was strapped up to the most powerful oxygen machine that exists, but it still wasn't enough to keep her heart rate regulated below 130 beats per minute. To put it in perspective, it's like she was running on a treadmill while trying to breathe through a straw, for two weeks.

It was painful to watch.

The doctors explained that when patients receive a terminal diagnosis like this, they typically prescribe morphine to keep them comfortable while dying. The only problem with that option, however, was that while the morphine would take away the pain, it would also put mom to sleep. The idea, according to the doctors, would be that our mom could drift into death without feeling anything.

To be honest, seeing how hard she had to work to stay alive made this option seem viable to all of us. But mom would have nothing to do with it. She ardently rejected any morphine under any circumstance.

The doctors were dumbfounded. They didn't understand why someone going through so much pain would refuse the very medication that could take that pain away.

The issue for Mom was not that we would be there with her but that she wanted to be there with us. She wanted to stay conscious so she could be fully present with her family in her last few moments on earth.

Having been a nurse herself, she saw the way morphine removed a person's ability to fight. And fight she did, right up to the very end.

Looking back, it was a little crazy how it all went down. There were times when her oxygen levels would dip so low that her lips started turning blue. The machine buzzer would go off and the nurses would come in and try to get her back to normal. Each time that happened, the palliative doctor (the one who's supposed to help you die well) would come in and offer Mom morphine.

"NO!" she would grunt out, barely able to voice the word.

By this point, all of us kids were in agreement. "Mom," we said. "It's okay to take morphine. We'll be here with you."

While her family and medical staff offered solutions to stop her from feeling *pain*, Mom continued to resist anything that would keep her from feeling *us*.

The last few days of her life were the most sacrificial picture of love we had ever seen. We saw Mom endure such immense pain just so she could be with us—so she could hold our hands, hear our voices, listen to worship music with us, and catch a glimpse of each grandkid when she could muster the strength to open her eyes.

On the last night of her life, my daughter, Allie, and I slept in the hospital room with her. We made a pallet on the floor behind her bed. Allie was such a trooper. She stayed up all night long to be with her, helping adjust her mask or get her a drink—whatever she could do to make her Nana comfortable.

At this point, Mom hadn't said much for three days.

At about one o'clock in the morning, I woke up and saw Allie leaning over the bed just staring at Nana while holding her hand. Mom's oxygen levels had dipped so low I thought it was only a matter of minutes before we would lose her. But at that moment, right when I thought mom was completely unconscious, I heard her grunt out in the faintest voice, "I ... love ... you ... Allie."

She could barely get the words out, but I heard it. Even more importantly, Allie heard it.

Mom died that afternoon. But not before she gave her granddaughter an experience that will mark her life forever, something she will cherish until the day she goes to be with Nana in Heaven.

Mom showed us the *power of presence* and the sacrifice it takes to have it. In the last moments of her life, amidst incredible pain, she gave us the greatest gift she could ever give—herself!

Do you know what your spouse wants from you more than anything? YOU!

When you are fully present, you become a wonderful *present*—a priceless gift to your spouse.

But it's going to require sacrifice. You may have to cut that meeting at the office short. You may have to put your phone down, miss the big night out, or refuse to let your mind wander when your spouse is repeating the same thing you heard yesterday.

Whatever it is, the sacrifice is worth it in the end.

Being fully present sends a powerful message to your spouse that they are the most important person in the world to you.

My dad always told my brother and me, "Boys, wherever you are, be all there."

My mom lived what my dad taught. Her example inspires me to practice presence. The sacrifices I have to make seem so small compared to hers.

Let's follow my mom's example together.

HONEY DO:

This was a tough one to write. Hopefully, my laptop's keyboard will recover from the water-works! The only thing I want you to do today is find your spouse and hug him/her. Then commit to being fully present whenever you're together. Our days are numbered, and we will never regret being fully present with those we love most.

QUIT QUITTING

"Remember that guy that gave up?
Neither does anyone else."

– Anonymous

Don't give up!

Most of us have heard the stat that approximately 50% of all marriages end in divorce. But what you might not know is that the average divorce takes place within the first seven years of marriage.[vi]

Think of how lame wedding vows would be if the couple said, "Until the seven-year mark do us part!"

In his bestselling marriage book *Sacred Marriage*, Gary Thomas said, "Experts suggest it takes from nine to fourteen years for a couple to truly create and form its being."

Many couples call it quits before they reach the point where they can finally start seeing their years of effort pay off! How tragic.

We've all felt the sting of difficulty in those first few years of marriage. But the truth is, marriage is tough no matter how long you've been hitched.

The ones that make it, however, are those who have a dogged determination to stick with each other no matter how hard it may get.

We're fans of the UFC (Ultimate Fighting Championship). I (Jason) more than Tori. Although she does like to watch certain fighters with their crazy antics.

In the UFC, a fighter can lose four ways:

- He can get knocked out.

- The ref can stop the fight (TKO).
- He can lose on the scorecard.
- He can tap out.

When a fighter taps out, he essentially quits the fight, yields to a stronger opponent, grants the victory to his challenger, and asks the ref to stop the action so he can leave.

Because of this, tapping out is the worst way for a fighter to lose. It's the same in your marriage. Tapping out is a losing proposition.

It's not just a loss for you and your spouse, but a loss for everyone—your kids, your family, friends, church, etc.

We read an anonymous quote years ago that captures a *don't quit* mantra:

Marriage is hard. Divorce is hard. Choose your hard. Obesity is hard. Fit is hard. Choose your hard.

Being in debt is hard. Being financially disciplined is hard. Choose your hard. Life will never be easy. It will always be hard. But we can choose our hard. Choose wisely.

When we made our vows back in December of 2000, we believed them to be just that—vows— promises that we would not break, period. We entered our marriage with an "I won't quit on you no matter what" attitude.

And we're certain you did, too.

But quitting isn't just about divorce. Couples can stay married but quit the relationship. They can stay related but give up on trying to connect. This is just as devastating.

In either case, couples who quit not only give up on themselves and their spouse, but they also quit on the God who has the power to transform their relationship.

Studies show that 76% of couples who choose to stick it out can experience complete marital satisfaction and fulfillment within five years. If you stick with it and refuse to give up, there's a reward on the other side.

So don't quit!

Tapping out on your relationship tells God He's not big enough to fix your problem. That's a lie. He's big enough. You can trust Him and refuse to give up!

HONEY DO:

Take some time and discuss with your spouse if there's an area of your relationship where you've given up. Or maybe there's something you've hoped for in your marriage that isn't coming to fruition, so you're tempted to quit. Spend some time together and open up to each other. Then re- commit to each other that you're in it for the long haul, no matter what!

RESTORE ROMANCE

*"To awaken human emotion is the
highest form of art."*
– Isadora Duncan

Remember when you dated and how fun it was to do romantic things together? A candlelight dinner at a restaurant, watching a sunset on the beach, enjoying a slow dance in the kitchen—it was so easy and natural to do back then.

Of course, then you got married and things changed a bit. While it's completely normal for the euphoric feeling of infatuation to dissipate in your relationship—it can be a good thing as it grounds you in reality—it's not good to lose that little spark that makes your marriage fun and exciting.

So, here's the question: do you want more romance in your marriage?

If we have learned anything in our relationship, it's this - *change starts with desire.*

If you don't want to restore romance to your marriage, you can rest assured it won't happen. But if you really want it, you can certainly have it.

Let's get practical.

If we're going to restore romance, we need to answer three questions:

1. What is romance?
2. Why is it necessary?
3. How do we get it back?

Let's start with *what*. Romance is defined as "a feeling of excitement and mystery associated with love." Romance is first and foremost a "feeling." It's an emotion.

An emotion is "an impulse to act." Our emotions make us *feel* something so we want to *do* something.

What is the feeling of romance? Excitement and mystery.

Excitement is that little butterfly feeling in your stomach before your wife walks out of the bedroom in the new dress she got for your anniversary dinner, or that eager desire to be intimate with each other after an extended time away.

Mystery looks like consistently searching and exploring each other in search of deeper treasure, knowing there is always more to be found.

Romance is a mindset. It's a way of thinking, feeling, and acting.

So *why* would the excitement and desire of romance be necessary in a marriage?

Plain and simple, romance connects you more deeply with your spouse. And the closer your connection, the stronger your marriage.

We were designed for connection. There is something inside every human being that longs for it. Romance offers a unique connection that is exclusive between you and your spouse. It's special and should be valued as such.

Romance turns a friend into a lover. And, in the context of marriage, it's important to be both. A relationship void of romance is simply a friendship.

The question now is, *how* do we become more romantic?

If you want to be a true romantic, you need to consider two things:

- The atmosphere you create
- The things you do

When it comes to creating a romantic atmosphere, you need to engage one or more of the five senses: sight, sound, smell, taste, touch. Our bodies naturally respond to certain stimuli, so the more of the senses you engage, the more romantic your experience will be.

Dim lighting (sight), soft music (sound), scented candles (smell), gentle kiss (taste), slow dance (touch). These are all examples of a romantic atmosphere that can stir up your emotions and get you "into your feels."

We obviously can't live in that zone all the time. It's great for a special evening, but what can we do to keep romance alive in our everyday lives?

In his book *Marriage on The Rock*, Jimmy Evans gives us the answer. He teaches that romance is *fulfilling an unspoken need or desire in your spouse.*

According to Evans, if your spouse has a need or desire and you do something about it without them having to ask, that's romance.

When you operate romantically by engaging the senses when possible, and you consistently find something special and unexpected to do for your spouse, you can rest assured that you are going to feel something for each other.

That feeling is romance, and it's going to connect you on a much deeper level.

Romance was God's idea. He created it and gave it to us as a gift. All we have to do is open it up and use it.

Now you know how.

HONEY DO:

Remember back to something romantic you did when you were dating and do it again. Recreate it as best you can and feel those emotions. We did this in our kitchen a few months ago when the kids were gone; we turned off all the lights, lit some candles, ate dinner together with soft music in the background, and then danced to our favorite love song. It's amazing how you can stir your emotions when you're proactive like that. Try it out!

PRINCIPLE NINETEEN

PRINCIPLE NINETEEN
SAY SAY "YES" TO SUBMISSION

"The starting block for people who are going to stay in love is mutual submission."

– Andy Stanley

If a title that includes the word "submission" makes you nervous, don't worry; we're coming from a different angle than what you're thinking. Submission is a beautiful thing in marriage.

Did you know that the verse "wives submit to your husbands" is preceded by a verse that teaches us to "submit to *one another*?" (Ephesians 5)

And both of these verses come just before a set of instructions on how to put on the full armor of Christ.

If we need to put on armor, what does that presuppose?

It presupposes that we're in a fight. And the secret to success in this fight? Submission—to God and others.

Ephesians 5 & 6 is where these instructions are found. Within these power-packed chapters, Paul shows us the value of yielding to others and how it prepares us to engage in the spiritual battle we face.

Submission is "the action of accepting or yielding to the will or authority of another person." We submit to God first, and then we submit to others.

The two are linked in the same way that love is linked—loving God and loving others. If you want to show your love for God, then show it by loving others.

Submission works the same way. If we want to show our submission to God, then we do it by submitting to others. "Submit to one another out of reverence for Christ." (Ephesians 5:21)

The primary "other" in your life? Your spouse.

In terms of *structure*, submission is vertical. God placed man as the leader in the marriage and gave him full responsibility for the strength and health of the relationship. If things go south, God looks to the man first.

But in terms of *service*, submission is horizontal. God placed man and woman on an even playing field, and as we submit to each other out of reverence for Him, we get His blessing and protection.

I (Tori) know that God made Jason the leader in our home, and as he submits to God, I'm safe to submit to him. But Jason mutually submits to me in the way he leads. He operates in a "we" mindset, not a "me" mindset. He trusts and relies on my discernment in the decisions we make.

Choosing to submit to one another out of reverence to the God who put you together will take your marriage to new heights.

Mutual submission in marriage looks like habitually deferring to your spouse—preferring their thing over your thing. As Andy Stanley put it in one of his sermons, "Marriage should be a *submission competition*."

This was easy to do in our dating years. Our conversations back then sounded something like this:

"You go first." "No, you go first."

"You pick where we should eat." "No, you pick."

"What do you want to do tonight?" "Whatever you want to do." "If you like it, I like it." "I'm happy if you're happy!"

What marked those early years was a willingness to yield our own desire for the desire of the other. We did it without even thinking. It was the simple and natural way we interacted.

But what often happens in marriage is our self-preservation instinct kicks in and we find ourselves shifting from the mindset of *we* to the mindset of *me*. As a result, trust is broken; you no longer feel like your spouse has your best interest in mind.

Don't let that happen!

Fighting takes a lot of energy, regardless of who or what you are fighting. Mutual submission channels that fight inside of you for the good of your marriage.

That's what the concept of *Beauty in Battle* is all about. Fighting together draws you together when you establish your marriage on the foundation of submission—to God and each other.

Yielding to each other is a choice. But you'll see huge gains in your relationship if you do it.

HONEY DO:

Take some time to discuss with your partner what mutual submission in your relationship looks like. Are you both fully yielded to God in every area of life? Do you naturally yield to each other in the practical decisions of your marriage? If not, what can you do to fix it?

PRINCIPLE TWENTY
TRUST THE
TRIANGLE

*"What if God designed marriage to make us
holy more than to make us happy?"*
– Gary Thomas

Your marriage is not about you and your spouse; it's about you and Jesus. Marriage is the context in which we learn to *live* and *love* like Him.

We live like Jesus through service and sacrifice. We love like Him through forgiveness and restoration.

Marriage is the training ground to teach us these things. Christ serves, sacrifices, forgives, and restores those who've sinned against Him. And He calls and empowers us to do the same.

When you put your spouse's needs before your own and you serve them as best you can, you're living like Jesus. When you forgive your partner for wrong-doing and you seek restoration, you are loving like Jesus.

Marriage isn't about making you *happy* but about making you *holy*.

Did you know that your spouse was put into your life to make you more like Christ? And you were placed in their life to make them more like Christ?

Your marriage relationship is all about your God relationship.

That's what "Trust the Triangle" is about. When you learn to focus on God, you'll draw closer to your spouse. When you move toward God individually, you will draw close to your spouse relationally.

How does this work?

Picture a triangle with a point at the top and two points at the bottom. God is the point on the top. You and your spouse are the points at the bottom. As each of you focuses on God and moves toward Him, the closer you get to each other.

This is the way God intended your relationship to grow. The health of your marriage is determined by the health of your personal relationships with God.

We've counseled many couples throughout the years, and we've seen one thing to be exceedingly clear: there is no such thing as "marriage problems." There are only "God problems." And these problems, by and large, are the result of sin.

Somewhere, someway, somehow, one or both partners broke fellowship with God and allowed sin to creep its way in, which manifested itself in a strained or broken relationship.

If you solve your individual problems with God, it will solve your marriage problems with your spouse (so long as both partners commit to it).

Getting to the root of your marriage problem leads you to the problem of sin. In fact, one of the chief sin issues among the couples we've counseled is *idolatry*.

We know that sounds odd but follow us here. We're not talking about bowing down to a little wooden statue in your bedroom. We're talking about placing your spouse in a position in which only God was meant to be.

When a wife looks to her husband for ultimate fulfillment or a husband looks to his wife for the same, they are replacing God with their spouse. The Bible calls this idolatry.

If we allow the sin of idolatry to creep its way into our personal lives, we create a chain reaction of broken fellowship—first with God, then our spouse, then our family, and down the line.

Your spouse was not created to meet your needs—only God can do that. The way He chooses to meet your needs involves your spouse, but they are not the ultimate source—He is. We discussed this earlier in *Principle Twelve - Look To The Lord.*

When we put our trust in God more than our spouse, we no longer demand our needs to be met by our spouse, nor do we seek to get what we want when we want it. We simply let go and let God. We yield control of everything to Him by focusing on Him.

When you learn to "Trust the Triangle" by focusing on and drawing close to God individually, He will bless you relationally. You'll draw closer to God and your spouse at the same time.

As a result, not only will both of you look more like Christ, but you'll have a relationship that can truly bring Him glory.

HONEY DO:

On a scale of 1-10, where are you in your relationship with God in terms of the effort you put in? If there's room for improvement, what areas might you commit to strengthening? Secondly, have you been looking to your spouse to meet needs only God can meet? If so, commit to shifting your focus back to Him.

UNDERSTAND UNFORGIVENESS

"Not forgiving someone is like drinking poison and expecting the other person to die."
– Nelson Mandela

There's not a single marriage in existence where forgiveness isn't necessary. While there's beauty in the midst of battle, it doesn't happen apart from a few mishaps along the way.

The nature of relationships is that people make mistakes, and when the inevitable happens, forgiveness is the only thing that keeps you together.

Over the years, we've seen unforgiveness as one of the main issues that keeps couples from experiencing the power that God wants them to have in their relationship. Whether they need to forgive their spouse or someone outside their marriage, unforgiveness robs them of intimacy.

Below is an excerpt from our book where we talk about forgiveness in marriage—not just toward your spouse when they've wronged you, but from others in your past as well. Unforgiveness from the past is a trap that keeps you from living in the fullness of the present.

Forgiveness Redefined

When you refuse to forgive someone, you give them power over you. But if you forgive, not based on the person deserving it but based on God's forgiveness toward you, you are the one who is set free.

At the same time, blindly forgiving someone who hasn't repented can be equally destructive. In the Bible, we're told to forgive as God forgives. Does God forgive an unrepentant person? He … does … not.

God forgives those who repent—those who ask for forgiveness. They need to first feel condemnation for what they've done. Then, when they repent, God can and will forgive them.

God's justice is meant to lead people to Him. If we blindly forgive someone who hasn't repented, then we trample God's justice. Something in our hearts won't sit right.

So, what do we do when someone wrongs us but doesn't repent?

We certainly can't hold unforgiveness in our hearts; otherwise, we'd be sinning. Rather, we do what Jesus did when He was on the cross. He said, "Father, forgive them." (Luke 22:34)

Jesus had the power to forgive sins because He said to the paralyzed man, "Your sins are forgiven." (Mark 2:5) He saw the man's heart and could tell he was truly repentant. So, He granted forgiveness.

But on the cross, He knew those who took part in putting Him there were unrepentant. He had forgiveness in His heart and would freely give it to those who repented, but until they did, He gave the situation to God and let Him handle it. In the meantime, He was free.

Here's an easy way to keep it straight in your mind:

When someone (including your spouse) wrongs you and they repent, do what Jesus did with the paralyzed man—grant forgiveness. No matter how bad their sin against you was, your responsibility in light of Christ's great sacrifice is to grant them the same forgiveness God gave to you.

But when someone (spouse included) wrongs you and they don't repent, do what Jesus did on the cross—give the situation to God and let Him handle it. In the meantime, you stay "ready to forgive." This will keep you from walking around in unforgiveness, which will only harm you and those you love. In the process, you trust God to handle the situation.

Maybe this is something you're struggling with right now. Maybe the person has repented, and you need to grant forgiveness. Do it as Jesus did with the paralyzed man, understanding that the emotional scars will take time to heal. During that time, erect some boundaries to protect yourself and the relationship. These boundaries act like a cast on a broken bone, assuring that healing can take place.

If the person hasn't repented, do what Jesus did on the cross and give the situation to God. Do not blindly forgive. If you do so, then your sense of justice will be trampled on, and it won't sit right. Deep down, you'll know justice needs to be served. When you give the situation to God, you are releasing the issue and no longer holding onto unforgiveness. In this way, you will be free.

Apply this type of forgiveness in your marriage and watch how free you can be. "If the Son sets you free, you are free indeed" (John 8:36).

HONEY DO:

Is there someone who has wronged you in the past that you're having a hard time forgiving? If so, walk through the two scenarios above and set yourself free. If it's your spouse, do the same and bring them into the conversation.

PRINCIPLE TWENTY-TWO
VOICE VALUE

*"It's amazing how far you're willing to go
when someone believes in you."*

– Kate Kacvinsky

One of the greatest gifts you can give to your spouse is to believe in them.

The story of Gideon in the Bible captures this perfectly. He was a guy who struggled with fear and a lack of faith but fought through those natural inhibitions to lead the Israelites in one of the greatest military exploits of all time.

In Judges 6, we see the powerful Midianites terrorizing the powerless Israelites. When the Israelite farmers would harvest their crops, the Midianites would rush in and take it all, leaving them empty- handed. In response to their cry for help, God raised up an unlikely deliverer.

Knowing the job at hand was an enormous one, God had to first prepare Gideon for the task. As Gideon was threshing wheat, the angel of the Lord appeared and said, "The Lord is with you, O *valiant warrior*." (Judges 6:12)

Stop right there. Gideon struggled with fear and doubt big time. He was naturally fearful and had a hard time trusting God.

So why this salutation? At this point in his life, it appeared that Gideon was anything but valiant or a warrior.

But God saw in Gideon what Gideon didn't see in himself. He believed in Gideon and called out the man He wanted him to become.

God had to speak it into Gideon before He called it out of him!

And the rest is history. Gideon led 300 dudes against an army of 135,000 and by God's almighty power, he crushed them! All because God called a common man for an uncommon purpose by believing in him before he believed in himself.

What we mean by *voice value* is doing the same thing for your spouse that God did for Gideon.

One of the greatest gifts you can give to your spouse is to believe in them, to speak life into them, and to call out the man or woman God destined them to be.

I (*Jason*) know what this feels like firsthand. Many of you may remember when HGTV fired my brother and me back in 2014 for our stand on Biblical principles. If you haven't heard that story, you can read about it in our book *Whatever the Cost*.

From that time forward, we became public enemy number one for many activist groups. They attacked us and called us every name in the book, vilifying us in front of a watching world. It was a difficult time for us.

But while everyone saw us standing strong publicly, nobody saw what was going on privately, specifically with me. I feared the consequences of having my character assassinated and doubted what good could ever come of it all. But every time I was tempted to throw in the towel,

Tori would speak life into me and call out the warrior in me.

On one specific occasion, after HBO's Bill Maher did a hit piece on us and called us "nitwits who believed in a dumb book" to a laughing crowd, Tori came over to me and said, "I know the man you are. These people don't. Your strong stand gives others the courage to stand, too. You're showing them what bravery looks like. God raised you up for this moment. I'm so proud of you!"

She spoke so much life into me that I felt like I could attack hell with a squirt gun. With every word, I felt more and more like the warrior I knew God wanted me to be, despite the natural fear that threatened to take over.

The real beauty of that moment, however, was not just that Tori's life-giving words gave me the strength and courage to stand, but that they drew me closer to her than ever before. The more she built me up with her words, the more magnetized I was to her.

Because Tori *voiced value* to me, I was able, by God's grace, to stand for His truth publicly. I was able to face my fear and stand victorious over it.

I've heard it said that courage isn't the absence of fear; it's doing what's right in spite of it. My wife is the one who spoke that courage into me and then called it out of me.

And you can do the same for your spouse.

HONEY DO:

Think about the person God has called your spouse to be—even if they are not acting in alignment with it right now. Speak it into them and then call it out! Become the encouragement they need.

PRINCIPLE TWENTY-THREE
WALK IN WE-NESS

*"Alone we can do so little; together
we can do so much."*

– Helen Keller

When you're in it together, you win it together.

Several years ago, I (*Tori*) had a late-night conversation with our oldest son, Trae. It's funny how teenagers open up if you stay up late enough to catch them in a rare chatty moment. You take what you can get with teenage boys. Ha!

Trae is a Division 1 college basketball player now, but at the time of our conversation, he was a freshman in high school. He had just made the varsity team and was working hard to earn his spot. One night my brother, Zac, who happened to live next door, saw him shooting outside around midnight. Even though it was ice cold outside, Zac bundled up and rebounded for him.

A few days later, Trae got put into a really tight game, and by God's grace, he went off ! He was hitting three-pointer after three-pointer until his team won and he ended up with 22 points. I couldn't stop smiling when I heard the student section chanting, "He's - A - Freshman!"

But my mom-heart will be forever warmed by what I saw at halftime. As Trae was walking off the court, having just hit a last-second shot to end the half, Zac ran over to where he was and gave him a big hug.

"That's how you do it, Trae!" Zac yelled. "That's why you're shooting shots at midnight!"

Trae's face lit up like a Christmas tree. I could see the power of Zac's words filling up his love tank. A few days later, Trae told me how those words affected him.

"Mom," he said. "When Zac came up and hugged me at halftime, I felt like I wanted to cry. I have no idea why I felt so much emotion, but for some reason, I felt like Zac was in it with me, like he was in the game and we were doing it together. It felt really good."

Of course, I knew exactly what he was talking about. There's something incredibly powerful when you have a sense of "*we're in this together*" with another person.

Jason says it all the time—fighting together draws you together in marriage the same way it does in the military. When you get a few hundred guys together and put them in the middle of a battle, those strangers quickly become a band of brothers. There's no better sense of togetherness than when you're in a fight together.

That is what Trae was feeling that night, and it's one of the greatest gifts we can give to our spouse.

When your spouse knows that you are with them and will take their side, no matter what, it gives them that feeling of *us* that keeps your bond strong.

It's these "*I'm in it with you*" experiences that draw you close.

HONEY DO:

Think back to a time when your spouse gave you a feeling of "*I'm in this with you.*" How good did that feel? Has there been a time when you didn't feel that way? If so, discuss it with your partner, and determine to get it fixed!

PRINCIPLE TWENTY-FOUR
XPRESS THE XENIAL

*"When you are kind to others, it not only changes you,
it changes the world."*

– Harold Kushner

If you're lingually challenged like we are, you have no idea what the word *xenial* means. We had to look it up! But when we did, we discovered that it's really good for building a solid marriage.

Xenial is an adjective used to describe a "friendly relationship between two parties, in particular between a hospitable host and his or her guests."

Think about the last time you had guests over to your house. Like us, you probably did everything in your power to make them feel as comfortable as possible.

But have you ever had a situation where one of your guests spilled their drink on the floor or accidentally broke a plate or something? How did you respond? Did you lace into them with a verbal tirade that would make a sailor blush? Or did you accommodate them to not make them feel bad for their blunder?

Chances are good that you chose the latter.

If we treat our guests like this—people to whom we have not committed our heart and soul—why would we treat our spouse differently? Yet we often do.

Herein lies one of the dangers of being around someone a lot—it can breed *familiarity*.

You've probably heard the phrase "familiarity breeds contempt." We talked earlier about the dangers of contempt and did a recent podcast on the topic. When you're around someone a lot, it's easy to get frustrated at little things and get sharp with your interactions. The next thing you know, you're treating them like you would never treat a stranger.

But one of the worst things that happens when familiarity sets in is not that we get sharp with each other, but that we stop pursuing one another.

Familiarity causes us to stop hunting for that which we believe we've already found. We get so used to each other that we stop searching for those little nuggets of gold buried deep in the heart.

In dating, we searched for these things in our spouse with great precision and patience. But for many of us, when we said, "I do," the search was called off. Now, the treasures we are meant to find remain buried.

We have news for you: your spouse is a treasure chest just waiting to be opened. There's more good stuff in there than you'll ever discover in a lifetime of searching.

God wants you to know your spouse deeper and deeper. If you keep searching, just about the time you think you've got them all figured out, you will discover there's more in there.

When you approach your marriage like this, familiarity dissipates.

About five years into our marriage, I (*Jason*) realized that I was taking Tori for granted. We were as familiar with each other as two people could get, and while we weren't on the brink of divorce, we were a shell of what we once were—and a small fraction of what God intended us to be. The more I thought about it, the more it bothered me.

If you read our book, you know what God did to wake me up. While I don't have time to go into the whole story here, suffice it to say that God spoke clearly to me that conquering familiarity starts by pursuing Tori like I did when we were dating.

You'll notice that pursuit is a common theme in this book. As we've found in all our years of coaching, if we can get spouses to pursue each other again everything else falls into place.

Here's the cool part—when God sees you pursuing His son or daughter with a heart to draw close to them, He jumps in and helps out! We have to remember that God is not just our Father, but our Father-in-Law. So, when He sees our effort toward His son or daughter, it touches His heart in a deep way.

If familiarity has already set itself firmly in your relationship, your pursuit of each other will change things dramatically for you. But it doesn't just work in your marriage; it works with your kids as well.

This really hit home for me a few months ago when my youngest son spilled something on the floor. I was pretty sharp with him, as usual. But sitting there in silence as I watched him clean it up, my seven-year-old daughter, who's never short on words, spoke up.

"Daddy," she said in her cute little voice. "When mom spills something why do you say, '*Oh, it's ok sweetheart. I'll help you clean it.*' But when we do it you get mad?"

That one hit me hard. While I had conquered familiarity in my marriage, I hadn't defeated its power over my relationship with my kids.

That little rebuke set me straight. I've since committed myself to do the one thing that breaks the power of familiarity—*pursuit*—both with my kids and my wife.

So, if you find yourself more apt to be *xenial* with invited guests than your life partner, try attacking your familiarity with pursuit.

HONEY DO:

Today's a great day to take inventory of your marriage and ask yourself, "Do I take my spouse for granted? Am I still actively seeking to know him/her more deeply? Have I let familiarity creep its way in?" Whatever the answer, commit to pursuing your spouse like did before you got married. Oh, and include your kids in the mix as well!

PRINCIPLE TWENTY-FIVE
YIELD YOURSELF

"A good marriage is not a contract between a man and woman, but rather, a sacred covenant between three; the man, the woman, and God."

– D. L. Kauffman

The foundation of your marriage is the covenant you made with your spouse the day you stood at the altar and made your vows. It's not a *contract* where stipulations are given and each party agrees, but a *covenant* between you, your spouse, and God.

We heard a pastor say that "a covenant marriage means we are glued to each other through a joint commitment to God first."

Why is this important? Because in a world where divorce is rampant, those who understand the value of their covenant will stick it out no matter how difficult things may get.

Yielding yourself means committing to operate according to the covenant you made with your spouse on the day you wed.

A covenant marriage is about mutual *yielding*—to God first and then to each other. God takes covenants very seriously.

Consider how Bathsheba was referred to in the genealogy listed in Matthew 1. "David was the father of Solomon by Bathsheba *who had been the wife of Uriah*." (Matthew 1:6)

Right there in the opening of the New Testament, we see God reminding us that Solomon's mom, Bathsheba, had been someone else's wife. God never forgot the covenant between Uriah and Bathsheba as husband and wife. And it's recorded in Scripture so we wouldn't forget it either.

The promises we made to each other while at the altar weren't token lines we recited in front of family and friends. They were *vows* that God takes seriously.

In the Bible, a vow is a promise made to your spouse *and* God.

Understanding this powerful truth will drastically increase the strength of your marital bond. Why? Because it brings in the accountability we need when the going gets tough. We know we can't quit on each other because we promised God we wouldn't.

To be in a true covenant relationship, God has to be a part. A man and woman can have a union, but they cannot have true *communion* without God being in the mix. This is how the disciples were able to stay united even when all hell broke loose against them. Their *union* was based on *communion* with God.

Marriages are falling apart today because God isn't in the mix—because couples aren't operating by the covenant they made when they said "*I do*." But yours doesn't have to end up like this. Your marriage *won't* end up like this.

Yield yourself to God and your spouse by a stubborn refusal to give up on the vows you made and watch how God blesses you for honoring your covenant.

HONEY DO:

This was a more theological principle than many of the other ones, so today would be a good day to pray and remind God (your Father-in-Law) of the promise you made to His son or daughter on the day you wed and recommit to honoring your word.

ZERO IN ON ZANYISM

"Couples who laugh together last together."
– Dr. John Gottman

The premise of *Beauty in Battle* is that fighting together draws you together. When you learn to fight alongside one another in a spiritual battle rather than against each other in a personal war, you'll discover relational connection in a deep and powerful way.

But it's not just fighting together that draws you together; it's also laughter! Some good old- fashioned humor.

That's what being "zany" is all about. A zany person "acts the buffoon to amuse others." While we're not asking you to dawn a red nose and oversized shoes, we are saying that clowning around with your spouse and laughing together brings life and health to your relationship.

One of the best things you can do for your spouse is to be the person who can make them laugh. Why is laughter so important? Because it fuels your friendship. And friendship is the lifeblood of your marriage.

Do you know what best friends do together? They laugh. A lot!

God created laughter as a way to not only heal the pain in our hearts but also draw us closer to those with whom we laugh.

This is one of the first things that attracted me to Tori. Growing up as a twin, my best buddy was my twin brother, David. We not only looked identical, but we also found the same things to be extremely funny. There were times when we'd bust out in laughter just by looking at each other.

I remember thinking I'd never find someone who could make me laugh as hard as David. That is until Tori entered the picture. All through our dating years, I think we laughed more than we talked.

Little did we know that laughing together was drawing us together, not only romantically but as true companions, best buddies who enjoyed each other's company more than anyone else's in the world.

Scientists have now discovered the power of laughter and how healthy it is. Here's what one recent study said:

"Laughter is strong medicine—it draws people together in ways that trigger healthy physical and emotional changes in the body. Laughter strengthens your immune system, boosts mood, diminishes pain, and protects you from the damaging effects of stress. As children, we used to laugh hundreds of times a day, but as adults, life tends to be more serious and laughter more infrequent. By seeking out more opportunities for humor and laughter, though, you can improve your emotional health, strengthen your relationships, find greater happiness—and even add years to your life."

If you want a healthy personal and relational life, laughter is the antidote!

Laughter applied to marriage can be a miracle cure. One of its most powerful aspects is how it helps alleviate conflict.

When we counsel couples struggling with perpetual conflict, we always tell them about the power of humor to extinguish the anger that results from butting heads. If they can figure out a way to make each other laugh during a fight, it will cool the negative tension that can otherwise keep them apart.

We've applied this to our own marriage. When we get into an argument, one of us will almost always say or do something that makes the other laugh. It almost always calms things down. We still laugh about the stupid things we've said in the heat of arguments.

We shared a story on our podcast recently about how we got into an argument over money a few years into marriage. Tori got so mad she wadded up a five-dollar bill and threw it at me and yelled, "Wipe your butt with this!"

Wow. I was not expecting that.

So, I took the bill, unfolded it, and made a wiping motion as if I were actually doing what she told me to do. We burst out laughing so hard we forgot what we were even fighting about.

To this day, we use that line at times to break the tension. "Wipe your butt with this" is a hard line to say without laughing, and it certainly helps us calm the conflict.

God created laughter. He infused it with the power to heal our bodies, minds, and relationships. All we have to do is tap in and let it do its thing!

HONEY DO:

So how do engage your partner with laughter?
A great place to start is online. You're only one
YouTube video away from a good relation-
ship-bonding belly laugh. Whether it's Tim
Hawkins or Nate Bargatze doing stand-up
comedy, or old clips of Chris Farley on SNL,
you can find a way to laugh together. Remember what made you laugh when you dated and
do it again. Thank us later.

CONCENTRATE TO CAPTIVATE

"You have been the summary of my existence; my biggest weakness, my greatest strength. The weathers of my life start and end with you. You complete me."

– Sapan Saxena in *UNNS - The Captivation*

Apparently, the alphabet only has twenty-six letters. Since this is a thirty-day devotional, consider these last four a bonus! Who doesn't like a bonus, right?

There's a great verse in Proverbs for married couples: "Let your wife be a fountain of blessing for you. Rejoice in the wife of your youth ... may you always be *captivated* by her love." (Proverbs5:18-19)

Solomon was the writer, so his advice comes from a husband's perspective. But the principle is the same for wives as well. God's best for your marriage is that you remain "captivated" by your spouse.

Captivate means "to attract and hold the attention of someone by being extremely interesting, exciting, pleasant, or attractive."

To *be captivated* is to find your spouse interesting, exciting, pleasant, and attractive.

Isn't this how we all felt when we dated? But then we got married and, while we still like each other and are attracted, the passion of being *fully captivated* begins to wane.

But it doesn't have to be that way. The verse above tells us it *shouldn't* be that way. So how do we remain captivated in marriage?

By changing the way we think. Captivation is all about *concentration*.

What you choose to think about your spouse will either draw you toward them or push you from them.

For example: Since I (*Jason*) was a kid, I've have had serious OCD tendencies toward orderliness. My room was always neat and tidy growing up, and I absolutely despised clutter and mess.

Then I fell in love with someone who was my polar opposite.

When we were dating, her messy room wasn't a big deal at all. What did I care that her closet looked like the Tasmanian Devil's cave? I thought her laid-back, spontaneous personality was cute and fun. It was the opposite of me, and it drew me to her.

Then we got married and I grew critical of the things I used to think were cute. The more I focused on the things I didn't like about her, the more I found I was no longer captivated by her the way I once had been.

Ultimately, I didn't have a Tori problem. I had a Jason problem. My focus was off.

When we were dating, all I thought about was what was right with Tori. But now that we were married, I focused on what was wrong. When dating, I'd thought about what I wanted to *give*. But after marriage, my thoughts gravitated to what I wanted to *get*. I wanted to get our room cleaned up so I could relax! It was all about me.

The girl who once captivated every part of me now frustrated the life out of me. I didn't realize that the secret to captivation is *concentration*.

Tori had captivated me while dating because I concentrated on the good in her rather than the bad. But after we got married, I flipped the two and began to concentrate on the bad and not the good.

This is something that happens in a lot of marriages.

Satan is our adversary who makes accusations for our agreement. His accusations come in the form of negative thoughts. We cannot agree with these thoughts; otherwise, we give them power over us.

When negative thoughts of Tori's "issues" entered my mind, I needed to refuse to give them the control they wanted. Practically, this meant concentrating on the good and not the bad.

Thinking positively about a person bonds you with that person. Our brains are wired for love. Neuroscience confirms this. Our bodies and minds function best when we choose loving thoughts.

God showed me that my job as a husband was to proactively think positive thoughts about Tori, to intensely focus on the things I love about her. By doing this, my interest, excitement, and attraction toward her would grow.

Here's the real beauty: when you're captivated by your spouse, the things you could easily criticize actually become cute.

Tori's almost as much of a neat freak as I am now, but I can honestly say that on those rare occasions when I walk into our closet and see her dresser drawers wide open, I'm reminded of what I love most about her. It makes me grin to think about her frantically getting dressed for church and not thinking twice about pushing the drawers in.

Isn't that crazy? Only God could transform an obsessive-compulsive punk like that. Such is the power our minds have over our emotions.

God wants you to remain captivated by your spouse. But the only way it will happen is if you intensely focus on what's good and not on what's bad.

Your concentration will lead to your captivation.

HONEY DO:

What are the great things about your spouse you can commit to concentrating on so that you can become captivated once again? Be proactive and think those thoughts today. Oh, and maybe share a few of them with your spouse as well!

LOOK THROUGH A NEW LENS

"If you want small changes in your life, work on your attitude. But if you want big and primary changes, work on your paradigm."

– Stephen Covey

Ｈow you see determines how you act. When perception changes, behavior changes.

The single best thing we've ever done for our relationship was to change the way we viewed it.

Our goal is not to simply give you how-to advice that focuses on behavior change. We want to give you a new lens through which you can view your spouse and the relationship you have together.

We've seen firsthand the power of this shift in perspective in our own marriage, and we've seen it happen to others in the process of our marriage coaching. As we counsel couples sitting on our living room couch, we've discovered that if we can get them to see differently, their behavior toward each other will change naturally.

Lasting change in marriage is only possible when you change the lens through which you view your relationship. The beauty of changing the way you see is that your behavior will change as a natural outgrowth of this shift in perspective.

This is what took place for us. We'd read lots of "how-to" books on marriage and put their advice into practice. Much of it was helpful, yet our behavior modifications were short-lived. We'd always drift back into old, negative behavior patterns. This outside-in approach that was aimed at changing behavior, while helpful to some degree, did not give us the lasting change we needed.

It wasn't until we changed the way we saw our relationship that we experienced the depth of intimacy we now enjoy. We no longer had to "try" anymore because our behavior changed from the inside out.

When we saw differently, we felt differently, and our actions followed naturally. The way you *see* influences the way you *feel*.

And the way you *feel* influences the way you *act*.

We read a story about a businessman on the subway in New York City who was peacefully riding to church one Sunday morning. Then a dad with three small kids entered the subway car. The moment they stepped in, the kids started yelling, throwing things, and running around the car—upsetting the once-peaceful atmosphere.

Clearly agitated, the businessman looked over at the dad and said, "Sir, your children are disturbing people. I wonder if you couldn't control them a little more?"

The dad looked up as if he were surprised at his kids' behavior. "Oh, you're right," he said softly. "I guess I should do something about it. We just came from the hospital where their mother died about an hour ago. I don't know what to do, and I guess they don't know how to handle it either."

At that moment, everything changed. This flustered businessman who had seen these kids as obnoxious and the dad as oblivious now viewed them through a lens of compassion rather than frustration. As a result, he was no longer angry but broken over their situation. This new perspective propelled him to offer his help.

Although nothing in the situation had changed, everything was different once he knew the truth behind the circumstances.

We want you to see your relationship differently, as the businessman did on that subway. We want you to see what God says about marriage and what He feels about your partner.

When you see your spouse as God's gift to you, someone who was made to be your ally, not your enemy, and how He has created them with a distinct personality laced with differences from your own so that you can accomplish His purpose for your life and relationship, everything changes!

When you see like this, your actions will change. And when your actions line up with God's intentions, He brings transformational power to your life and marriage.

The relationship we share today is living proof that change is possible and probable when this truth comes into focus.

You might think this kind of paradigm shift is impossible. Perhaps you and your spouse have developed deep-rutted routines over time that have you gritting your teeth and facing off against your partner about daily issues, large and small.

Truth is, God is just as excited to rekindle that romantic flame in your relationship as He is to raise the dead and heal the sick. He is all about mending broken things and bringing the Kingdom of God into your marriage.

When you see your spouse the way He does, He will breathe new life into your relationship.

HONEY DO:

Do you see your spouse for who they really are—a gift from God specially designed for you? Do your thoughts align with this truth? Do you see your relationship as God's way of manifesting His kingdom on the earth? If you change the way you see, we guarantee you'll see transformation in your marriage.

CRUISE THROUGH CONFLICT

"Conflict is inevitable. But combat is optional."

– Max Lucado

We talk about conflict a lot, but it lies at the heart of what we teach couples. Fighting together draws you together when you learn to embrace conflict rather than run from it.

Why would a good God allow conflict when He could easily take it away? Because conflict makes us more like Him.

It accomplishes the task by showing us what's inside—the stuff that's settled deep in our hearts, which we might not even be aware of.

Insecurities from our past can easily hinder us from becoming more like Christ. But when our eyes are opened, we can move toward healing.

This is captured beautifully in the movie *Beauty and the Beast*. The Beast tells Belle she can explore everything in the castle "except the west wing." Naturally, her curiosity gets the best of her. She goes exploring in the very place she was told not to go. While inside, she discovers clues about the Beast's past, a magical rose, and a room full of destroyed furniture pointing to a saddened and angry Beast unable to control his emotions.

The west wing is the epicenter of the Beast's insecurities. Thoughts of his past haunt him. But rather than deal with the reality of what happened and move toward emotional healing, he keeps this part of his life tucked away. As a result, the strength of the beast is used to hurt rather than heal.

The whole story revolves around this central issue: if he would only open up and let Belle bring healing to his wounded heart by revealing his sordid past, it would unlock him to become the prince he was meant to be.

Belle's wandering into the west wing caused an intense conflict between the two. But on the other side of this clash, we see a prince emerging from the Beast.

If Belle had never gone in there, if she had tried to avoid the conflict rather than lean into it, we never would have discovered the beauty within the Beast. He would have remained an angry animal fueled by the tragedy of his past rather than a soft-hearted and charming prince whose pain ultimately changed him for the better.

Here's the key: conflict had to take place for us to see the best in the Beast. And Belle was the one for the job.

That's what conflict in marriage does. It stirs things up in our hearts, the stuff that's buried deep inside, so that we can become the people God wants us to be and have the marriage God wants us to have.

To make this point even clearer, let's switch from a movie to a metaphor. Picture a cup of water with sand at the bottom. The water is clear. That is until you take a stick and stir it up. The minute the stick goes into the cup and the sand gets disturbed, the once crystal-clear water is nothing more than a muddy mess.

It wasn't the stick's fault. The stick simply revealed what was already at the bottom.

All of us have hearts that are like this cup: everything looks fine until we get stirred up, at which point we realize all the junk that was lying dormant at the bottom.

Your spouse is the stick God uses to stir you up. Imagine that. God uses the person you love the most to stir up things in you that He likes the least—things that are hindering you from becoming more like Him.

And He uses you as the stick to stir your spouse up, just as Belle did for the Beast.

Here's the deal: most of us have no clue how our past affects our present until we get married. We keep pain and wounds from long ago buried deep inside, resting somewhere in our subconscious. In time, we may even forget they're there.

But if we learn to lean into conflict rather than turning away, and we embrace the role of our spouse as God's tool to help us see what's buried down deep, we'll discover how conflict can make us healthy and draw us close at the same time.

So, when the sparks begin to fly (and they will), just know this is God's way of using your spouse to help you become more like Him and, ultimately, give you the marriage you truly desire.

HONEY DO:

Take some time to reflect on your relationship. Do either of you have a "west wing" that's out of bounds for the other to go? Do you have pain or hurt from the past that's sabotaging your present? Oftentimes, these things are revealed by perpetual conflict—areas of your relationship that have become sticking points. Talk this through with your spouse.

WIN THE WAR

"You cannot have a positive life and a negative mind."
— Joyce Meyer

We have news for you: As a married couple, your love story is couched in the middle of a war—a cosmic battle between the forces of good and evil. Satan hates everything about you because you're made in the image of the One that he hates above all others.

But it's not just you he hates; he can't stand your marriage. Why? Because your marriage reflects the relationship between Christ and the Church, two of his greatest enemies.

So he attacks, doing everything in his power to break apart the union God created to properly reflect His image.

But God promises that we, as couples, can be victorious over Satan if we simply trust in Him and stick together. Fighting together draws us together.

Understanding that we're in a spiritual war and we need each other to win the battle has been the single greatest unifier in our marriage.

We've said it before, but it bears repeating—the warfare for your marriage takes place on the battleground of your mind. Winning this battle is a matter of winning in your thoughts.

If Satan can get us thinking negatively toward our spouse, he wins. We lose. Here's a phrase we use to keep us in the winner's circle:

Satan is your *adversary* who makes *accusations* for your *agreement*. If you want to win, you must *refuse to agree with the accuser!*

Let's unpack this.

First, you must know that Satan is your *adversary*. He is your opponent who wants nothing more than to take you and your marriage down. He stands ardently opposed to everything good in your life, especially your marriage.

Second, Satan is your adversary *who makes accusations*. Here are the two main accusations Satan uses:

- <u>Accusations against yourself.</u> Satan doesn't want you to feel loved and accepted by God or others, so he throws negative thoughts into your head about yourself.

- <u>Accusations against others.</u> Satan hates relationships, so he breaks them apart by throwing negative thoughts into your head about others (especially your spouse).

An accusatory thought could sound something like this: "I don't have any good friends. I think I'm just too awkward for people to like me." Or: "My husband cares more about his job than me."

These kinds of thoughts are lies, but we only give them power when we *agree* with them. That's phase three.

Satan is your adversary who makes accusations for your *agreement*.

When you're tempted to believe a negative thought about yourself, you have to choose not to agree with that thought. Even when Satan reminds you of your past and tries to get you weighed down by guilt, don't give in to that faulty thinking.

When you're tempted to believe a disparaging thought about your spouse (or anyone else), you must do the same. Even if that thought contains some factual information, it won't ultimately lead to truth. The truth is, you and your spouse love each other and need one another.

Here's how you win: *Refuse to agree with the Accuser!*

When you properly understand your adversary is an accuser who simply needs agreement to thrive, you can refuse to give that agreement by countering his lie with the truth.

Tori had to do this a few months with me when I fell asleep in the middle of a late-night conversation (yeah, I know; it's bad). Early on in our marriage, if something like this happened, she would buy into Satan's accusatory thoughts—"Jason doesn't care about me. If he did, he'd be awake right now!" Then we'd end up arguing about it.

But Tori didn't get mad at me. Why? Because she refused to agree with the accuser. Tori recognized the truth wasn't that I didn't care about her when I fell asleep; the truth was that she'd picked the wrong time! I'd fall asleep on the president if he wanted to meet with me after 10:00 p.m.

So, when the negative thoughts come your way, recognize that they come from the Accuser who wants your agreement, and refuse to give it to him.

Instead, agree with God and counteract the lie with the truth. That's how you'll win the war in your relationship.

Oh, and I've since discovered that a 15-minute power nap keeps me awake for Tori's late-night convos. Win-win!

HONEY DO:

Have you given in to any accusatory thoughts against yourself? How about your spouse? Have you struggled with negative thinking toward others? If so, recognize that those thoughts come from Satan, and he wants nothing more than your agreement. Don't give it to him!

FINAL NOTE

Thank you for taking the time to go through these principles. You've done your part. Now, as you apply each of them to your marriage, watch how God will do His part.

Remember, God isn't just your Father, He's your Father-In-Law. So as you pursue His son or daughter with your whole heart, it touches Him in a special way.

Before we close, we want to leave you with one final thought. It comes from something God spoke to Jesus just before He went into the wilderness to be tempted by Satan.

God said, "This is my Son, whom I love; with Him I am well pleased" (Matthew 3:17). God said three things very clearly to His Son:

You're mine: "This is my Son…"

I love you: "…whom I love…"

I like you: "…with Him I am well pleased."

One of the greatest things you can do for your spouse is to let them know - through your words and actions - the same thing that God did to Jesus:

You're mine!

I love you!

I like you!

Pause for a moment and think about this. Is it true? Do your words and actions make your spouse feel like they're yours, you love them, and you like them?

We believe they do. The fact you went through this 30-day journey with us tells us that it's true. Your marriage is a powerful thing. Satan can't stand it. It's why he wages war against you, trying everything in his power to tear apart the relational bond you have.

But you can win. You *will* win. As you stand shoulder-to-shoulder with your spouse and apply these principles to your relationship, you will have a marriage that will last into eternity. And one day, we'll all be together participating in another marriage - one that takes place in Heaven between Christ and the church. If you're lucky, you might even see the two of us swing-dancing on the dance floor!

Now doesn't that sound fun? Let's do this together,

Jason & Tori

P.S. Whenever you're ready, here are a few ways we would love to help you strengthen YOUR marriage:

Beauty In Battle Book

If you haven't read our book already, you can get it anywhere books are sold.

Beauty In Battle Marriage Podcast

Join us weekly as we discuss all things marriage. We also share our favorite love song for the week and Tori's latest and greatest recipes!

5-Day Marriage Challenge

It's free and it's fun! And we promise that if you do the assignments in this short challenge, it will deepen your connection.

Marriage Bootcamp

Our flagship 12-part course where we share the exact framework we've used to connect relationally by fighting together spiritually (use code BIB50OFF for ½ off).

Marriage Coaching

The greatest athletes of all time need a coach! You can work directly with us or one of our coaching couples to strengthen your marriage.

Visit our website at BeautyInBattle.com for more information. You can also follow us on socials @ JasonAndTori

NOTES

i   https://beautyinbattlepodcast.buzzsprout.
    com/1913512/10289511-communication-in-
    marriage

ii https://www.gottman.com/blog/turn-toward-
    instead-of-away/

iii https://5lovelanguages.com/quizzes/love-language

iv https://www.bccpa.ca/news-events/cpabc-
    newsroom/2018/is-negative-thinking-bad-for-your-
    brain/

v   The Seven Principles for Making Marriage Work, by
    John M. Gottman, PhD.

vi https://www.gottman.com/about/research/couples/

vii https://whateverthecost.com/

viii https://pastorvlad.org/about/

ix https://www.helpguide.org/articles/mental-health/
    laughter-is-the-best-medicine.htm